AF400609

FSC
www.fsc.org
MIX
Papier aus ver-
antwortungsvollen
Quellen
Paper from
responsible sources
FSC® C105338

PERRY E. WILLIAMS

OPEN EYES

Through my lens - A glimpse of my world

This is dedicated to whomever picks this up,
enjoys it and helps avoid making the same
mistakes in life I did.
— Perry E. Williams Jr. —

Dear reader,

I, as the publisher, may or may not agree with the content of this book, or parts of it, but it is and remains the unadulterated words of the author himself, edited as little as possible. I believe in freedom of speech and that the death penalty is wrong without any exception. There is a saying, "*You can tell the value of a society by how it treats the weakest of its members.*" I believe that to be true. That's why I give these members of society the opportunity to raise their voice. Most of them have undergone a transformation for the better. They have developed a mental strength in prison that we can't even imagine due to being locked up and forgotten about. Even after all these years they are still there; living, learning and rising beyond themselves. We can learn from them as much as they can learn from us. To silence one of them would be to silence all of us.

Stefan Heikens

© 2023 by Perry E. Williams / Stefan Heikens
Cover Design and Artwork: Stefan Heikens
Edited by: Nicole Niehoff
Herstellung und Verlag: BoD - Books on Demand, Norderstedt
ISBN: 9783743118454

DEDICATION

This book is dedicated to Christopher Young, Tai Chin Pryor, Derrick Frazier, Tony Egbuna Ford, Tomas Gallo and a few other selected few who believed in me enough to take time out of their lives to show me my self-worth, and that I have a purpose in life. Thank you!!!!

And for those that aren't with us anymore, I am going to do all that I can to make y'all proud, and that your sacrificed time isn't in vain.

PERRY

POEMS

FOREWORD

OPEN EYES is my soul laid bare. I cannot remember a time that things didn't deeply affect me. Although, I could never put it into words. So I punched and kicked walls. I've sworn, yelled, bit at the air; and, at my lowest point, tried to end it all. Today, I look at the toll on my body, my scars (inner and outer), and marvel at how I ever ended up in such dark places... and more importantly, how I ever came back from them. I have been incarcerated in prison for the majority of my life under the worst sentence possible: Death! Men with this sentence are relegated to a building that is segregated and isolated from all other prisoners. Thus, the people you meet are also faced with the same uncertainty. Over the years I've lost so many friends, and am so troubled by it. I don't know if I can ever emotionally bond in this place again. I've often asked guys who've been here longer than me how they do it. I've gotten numerous answers. Some discovered God. Some discovered themselves through meditation, art, crafts and creative writing. I've tried various forms of religion before turning to Christianity; giving my life to Christ and giving it meaning. I also discovered poetry and creative writing (the language that gives sound to feeling). The fists of my emotions strike the walls inside of me (trapped and wanting out), finally finding a means of expression. OPEN EYES is me, raw and uncut; free and unchained.

Perry

1...2....3...

I don't want to live no more.
I wish I would just die in my sleep
So I wouldn't have to deal with this hell.
But I wake up every single morning to fresh tor-
ture.
It is time that I take matters into my own hands.
I'll make me a rope and hang myself tonight.
In a few hours I will hurt no longer.
I just need to first write my mama,
My dad,
Shawna,
And all my friends.
And tell them that I just
Couldn't live another day like this.
Pray a final prayer and hope I don't end up in hell.
Get ready to fall,
I guess I'll do it
On the count of three.
Then I won't be around to experience anymore of
this agony
1...
2...
3...

Written late 2003/2004

ACCEPTANCE

No longer will I allow being accepted to tempt me.
It's just a distraction with all it's well-crafted
dreams, showing me that I still have a long way to
go.

I've seen all its different faces.
I've heard it's many voices,
But I'm on the path to a better life.
I now see that I have no other choice.

Its arms are cold and empty.
Its words don't sound good anymore
'Cause I've found my true self
Who loves me and has so much more in store for
me.

I have done a lot of foolish things.
For it's love and affections I couldn't keep,
But that's all in the past now.
No more years of useless seeking and crying in my
sleep.

Acceptance has left me with all the scars-
By displaying to the world all of my failings
and wrong turns that I have taken in life,
But has only succeeded in showing me that
The Creator loves and hasn't forgotten about me.

And when my days are over,
and I close my eyes,

I'll take the Creator's loving hands;
and let Him lead the way.

CHRISTOPHER YOUNG

In the eyes of the public,
Christopher Young is a heathen.
A degenerate. A heartless killer.
Someone who can't be rehabilitated.

Yet, in my eyes, he's the cream
Of the crop, a God amongst men,
And a diamond in the rough to name a few.

He's my brother, one who I've strived
To be like, yet pushes me to be better
Than he is, and to reach my full potential.

And, if it wasn't for him, I wouldn't be
Here today, after two failed attempts on
My life at my own hands.

Because he helped me see and believe
In what I didn't believe or see in myself.

So, in closing, Christopher Young
Is a giver of knowledge, wisdom
And understanding, and someone who
I wouldn't be the man I am today if
I wasn't blessed with meeting him.

This poem was also published in the book
MY EXPERIENCE by **CHRIS A. YOUNG**

CLOSURE

It didn't take long to get to my resting place.
It wasn't until death row found me,
Backed into a dead end street called "Capital Mur-
der Case."

A case that was the result
Of a pointless desired treasure.
But when a man lost his life
The last thing I felt was pleasure.

I can't justify my actions
And now I face dire ramifications.
I wasn't raised to hurt others.
Much less being [with] or someone who kills with-
out hesitation.

I'm, not by any means, an inspiration,
And I don't want to be viewed as such by another.
But, I pray that others learn from my mistakes,
And see that Matthew was a precious son,
someone's brother.

I ask the Creator for healing and closure
For all the people I've caused so much pain,
and even if I must die for my actions,
I hope they can see the sun shining after the rain.

There's hope for better days.
I just pray that love conquers hate.
But, know that if you live by the gun,

You'll be judged and possibly murdered by the State.

CONSCIENCE

None of us decided in advance that we wanted to come to jail or prison. We simply did a certain thing or things which we had to do, and which seemed proper to do; nothing more, nor less. If it is foolish to insist on living in harmony with one's conscience, so be it.

If my imprisonment/sentence has no end, I shall receive it all from the Creator as a make of love. If my oppressors take my life, my heart and my mind will never be enslaved. And, as they afflict me on this earth, my soul will reside in the world to come. If, or when they kill me, I shall sing with love as I make my way to the kingdom of my Creator. I am glad to suffer the pain sent since the reason for all comes from our Creator.

So, feel your conscience for it's your life.

CONSCIOUS OF SELF

It's not about trying to be-
It's all about just doing.
Because righteousness isn't manifested in what
We say or even in
What we envision
Ourselves to want to do.

It's about the continued
Application of positive living.

Because there comes a point in life
Where you should be giving to life,
And not simply taking from it.

As "We" all have done for far too long.
And it's time to live for those
We love, and those who love us back!

So, stay focused and positive,
But don't expect the road to be an easy one.
Stay conscious of self at all times!
Because it's easy to fall off the ledge,
As we all will at one point.
But, it is the belief in ourselves
As Gods and Earths
That will see us through!

9/27/15

CONTROLLING YOUR OWN LIFE

Is having the will to tell-
Straight and to the point,
Without sugarcoating it,
Or without excuses.

You don't never need or have
To sweeten up
Your life.
Nor do you need or have to
Sensationalize it.

You just simply need or have
To accept it,
And what has happened.
And, by accepting it,
And what has happened,
You're no longer helpless.

By doing that you can go on
And write a new chapter.

You can tear that chapter
Of your life
To another level.

You can be in control of it-
And not being the victim
Of past situations,
And reaching higher
Accomplishing more.

But, know and believe
That this all starts
With yourself.
That's not being selfish.
That's just being real.

If it's wisdom you want to pass on
To another,
You must first
Attain wisdom for yourself.

If you go back and view
Your past clearly and truly,
You will have the best shot at
Clearly and truly
Viewing your present —
And forging your future
In the light of
Good sense and love.

CREATOR'S ALWAYS WITH YOU

Even though life's situations have you down and out. Whatever ordeal lies before you, always remember that the Creator's always with you.

And, even when it seems as if there's no end to the pain and struggle, know that the Creator will never leave you.

For, in all that you do, it will bring peace and courage to know that the Creator's Always With You.

CRUELTY TO HUMANS

I know that a lot of people feel that we should be treated worse than we're being treated now. But, I feel that it is wrong for a person to treat a human being like a dog at the Humane Society that's waiting to be put down. If the form of the legal system don't help them win their case that they are wrongfully convicted of, and this system don't want to seem as if *they* are wrong, they hurry up and put us to sleep.

See, this system looks at us as if we're pit bulls, which are supposed to be the most vicious. And, if that's the case, since I've been living on this earth, there have been proven facts of dalmations, Rottweilers, German shepherds and even the cute little Chihuahua's, hurting people. Bu, they say that pit bulls take the case. See, they put dogs to sleep when people don't come and get them. We're different, though. They take the ones whose family can't afford a good lawyer, and do them the way they want to do them.

This place affects our families because of the fact that some of us only have ourselves and/or our parents. This situation puts a lot of strain on their hearts. And, it's hard for them to do a lot of things. When they do try to get something done, they get messed over by these lawyers who are supposed to work for us, but in the end we're being set up. Again, I go back to the dogs that are in the Humane Society. If you can, please go and have a look at them. Look at how they look. Can't nothing on this earth look more sad than a dog when they know they can't get help, and those who are in charge are going to put them down.

The question is: Why did they just take a dog off the street just because they was walking down the street, or could have run away from home? Oh, I can tell you why: They said to clean up the streets. So, they take them and put them in a cage just like us. Then, two or three weeks to a month later, if they aren't gone, they kill them. They inject them with the same chemicals they use on us when they execute us. Ain't that a shame? We get treated like dogs while we're here, and then they kill us just like dogs when they feel that the time's up.

Has anybody ever thought about going to the place where some of us lived? Has anybody ever thought about why some of these people just let them do what they want to do to them?

The answer is NO! No one has gone to see what's going on in the places. I can tell you this, from the heart and experience, it does not feel good to see your family crying and heartbroken behind you being sentenced to die. And, knowing that you are the reason behind it, even if you didn't have anything to do with it.

Now, I don't know about a lot of you, but I love my family and would never want them to be hurt. Yet, these folks know what is going on and all they care about is getting people down here so that they can keep having a good record of executing people in this state. This is the most crooked state of all. All they want is somebody to put it on and they make sure that they get you. They know that you can't fight with them when the lawyer is on their team.

Please help save the lives of a lot of first time offenders and innocent people. Please!!!!!

A CRY FOR HELP

If you would only take the time
To lose yourself in my eyes
You might just get a glimpse
Of all the pain and misery that l hold inside
You would see that when it reaches its prime
I want to end my existence
And roll up and die
Self-inflicted murder;
l'm talking suicide
A short painless ride
Over to the other side
To a place where all suffering will finally subside
This is my little secret
Something that I hide
But since it's you
I guess 1 can confide
Hoping that you'll be able to turn the tide
And help me to find my stride.

Written in late 2003/2004

DEAR MAMA

Dear Mama,
As I reflect back on
The years we shared,
And all of the memories we've made,

All I see is you,
And the love you have for me.
That has helped me get through
Those days. Without your love

I would have never been
Able to carry on.

And today
As we see and speak
To each other,
Though there's glass
In between,
I always
Remember and consider
How lucky I am
To have a mother like you.

And though there's glass
in between,
We're so close,
But yet, so far away.

Always remember
That you'll always

Be my Mama,
And that I'll always
Love you beyond afar.

DELIGHTED

Silence suits me.
I am shrouded in quiet,
Cool serenity
Like the chill caress
Of marble against
A beloved cheek.
I am one with death.

I could meet beloved souls
As they leave.
Like Azrael;
I could be your
Long, lost friend,
Your sister,
Your mother,
Your brother,
Or your father's
Welcoming arms.

I am that much love...
I am wrapped up and drowned in love.
Ecstasy to the point of agony...

Silence suits me.
It is more fitting
Than the quiet scream in my soul:
I Love You, Creator!!!

Who could bear that torturing endearment???
As I am being boiled alive,

Inside my skin, my heart
Is being roasted like a suckling pig;
Sweet and juicy silence
Like a hot kiss in darkness.
The feel of our beloved arms,
I am being consumed by passion, love,
And silence more than being.

I love you more than life,
So let me die quietly,
And quickly, if I must,
S0 that I can become you;
Us!!!!!

DIALOGUE

Life is what it is, but as a brother wrote to me years ago, "The only time you should look down on someone is when you're bending down to pick them up." That is how it should be. I try to lead and follow the example that was set with me through him to the best of my abilities (even though he's been executed).

Even though those of us here haven't met up under the best circumstances, I try to deal with those that I deal with as I would my own brother or sister until they show me that I shouldn't. The way I think has both changed and matured, and I see things differently today than I did five or six years ago. I know and understand that we all face and endure things and pain in different ways. But I also know, yet I don't like, how we let those around us or our circumstances play a role into how we deal with things.

By that, I mean that if we aren't around someone who we feel that we can really talk to or feel that our particular circumstances are unchangeable, then we handle things the way we feel we need to, even though we may know inside that it's not the best way. But having someone is helpful, and the feeling that we can change things is what we need at times.

Being a 'better man or woman' has nothing to do with how we deal with pain, et cetera. Just because I don't handle things as others may handle things doesn't mean that I'm being the best man that

I can be. I see now that we are who we are at the moment when the struggle is upon us. Being a man or woman is about not just handling things, but about sometimes not handling them as well. For, we are all imperfect and will stumble along the way. Our strength builds us and becomes greater as we continue to get back up on our feet after we stumbled. Feel me?

So, in life, please never allow no one to ever make you feel less of yourself because we all move at our own pace. This world and place is full of fools who like to talk like they got it all figured out, but they don't. We all have to face our demons at our own time and our own pace.

It's true, we cannot control everything and we shouldn't allow ourselves to stress out over those things, but try to control and change all that we can, which starts now.

EXECUTION DATE

Darkness overtakes thee-
Fills thee with pain
That seems hard to maintain.

Weary the hours are
As thee tries to sustain.
Watching for the rays
Of light
To wash away the pain.

Yet, darkness continues
To overflow thee
With fretful pain.

As the key to the universe
Thee seeks
Frequently evades.

'Cause this key
will open the archway
Of light.

Where neither
Darkness nor pain
Can reside.

Written on Deathwatch 2015/2016

A FATHER

You're the reason
For my existence in life,
And if it wasn't for your love
I wouldn't be able to maintain.

Because I only wish
To be the best son
That I can
From which you
Can be proud of

Where everyday
Is a promise
Of greatness and fatherhood.

And I will always cherish
You as my father
Beyond myself
Because without you
There's no me.

Happy Father's Day, Pop! Written in honor of my Father

FIRST LADY

As I fade off to sleep,
I pray to the Creator my soul he keeps.
And Mama, even though I can't physically hold
your hand,
I mentally hug you.

You're delivered from heaven
Because even when I mess up,
You being my mama has made
My life so much better.

It's such a joy to
Hear and see you.
If you look in
The dictionary under the definition of *Queen,*
It would have your picture by it.

And every time I see you,
Or look at your picture,
I become mesmerized by the love
You have for me. When
I think I can't smile,
You smile that smile of love you have,
And all becomes clear.

If I never get to say it anymore,
I want you to know
That I love and care.

You could have been many other things,

But the Creator blessed me
And made you
My First Lady.

THE FORCE OF LIFE

I know that the
Pathway of life
Might be
Rough and difficult,
But always seek
The Glory of the Creator's
Loving life.

Stretch your mind
Higher and soar
Into to the
Glorious light
Of the spiritual sun.

Because I know that
This light is
A force
That flows through you,
Causing every
Adversity and struggle
To leave you
And make things right.

HEART

A peerless composition
Of a heart
Sojourn in time;
Composing barriers
Incapable of retreat.

Restrain your heart
Or your heart will restrain you.

And then you'll be inept
to demoralize
The barriers it
Has composed.

I KNOW NOT

I know not
Where this road
Before me will lead me,
But I know that the Creator
Will watch over me.

I know not
The fears or worries
Of what
Might become
Of my life,

But I know that the Creator
Is the controller of my life.
I know not of
Struggles or pains,
But I know that the Creator
Is near,
And will shelter
And
Protect me.

I know not
Where this road
Before me will lead me,
But I know that my soul
Will rest
Peacefully and eternally
In his loving arms.

I NEED A HUG

I'm on death row where they show us no love…as everybody waits on that lethal cocktail drug. My mind is playing tricks on me that I think they got hits out on me! In this cage I get lonely… I think about the abuse of wanting to be accepted that I've experienced throughout my life; that I've been ashamed to truly show my face...Now, the pain has taken up most of my space! l pray for better days, but the Creator sends no love my way! I got people saying that they love me, but they only love to hate me. Everybody has run out on me when it's time to stand by me. I've learned over the years to trust no one...Never fall in love 'cause it will only be viewed as a game. l thought I had someone that I can call my own, but it was just another bad dream. I take everything seriously, and live everyday as if it's my last 'cause I don't know how long I'm gonna last. The only person I got in this world that really loves me unconditionally outside of my mother is me… and those few that's in my private domain and are a part of this struggle 'cause don't nobody else love us. They just want to judge us. I wish I could run. I wish I could hide from all this pain that I feel inside because..."I need a hug"!!!!!

INSIDE

l suffer much
Pain and affliction,
With hopes to rest soon.

The heartache
Is more than incarceration,
Drowned out by
My tearful tunes.

My mental wounds
Remain hidden,
While my heart cries out,
I never loved you before,
Yet now, I'll love you
When my time is through.

The moment my third eye revealed you,
Right then and there,
I surely knew,
That it went far beyond
Any form of my understanding,
As it's a fragment
That remains true.

l could never fake
What l feel,
But only express
What is real.

I'll never stay silent
Because truth
Needs to be revealed.

Because when you find it,
Embrace it,
Keep it deep inside your heart;
Chain it to your soul,
And link it like a body part.

Protect it like
It's already your own.

Honor it like a
Heavenly throne.
A priceless stone;
Let it shine,
And be well known.

IT'S ALRIGHT TO MISS ME, BUT KNOW THAT I HAVE TO GO

The time has come
For me to end this journey,
And for dusk to
Set from dawn.

I don't want any tears shed,
And why should there be?

When I'm going to the universe
To my Creator
Where my soul
Can be set free!

It's alright to miss me,
But not for long.

And never with your head
Held down low.

Remember the
Love and memories
That we once shared,
And always keep me close,
But know that I have to go.

Dedicated to my father: Perry, Sr. - 2012

KIND WORDS FOR A FRIEND

Last night, I had thoughts of meeting someone like you while captured within my dreams. Hoping that you could feel my pain, even though I have nothing, but "Kind Words For a Friend".

Can you embrace this vision? Thinking, while you're listening, as I continue struggling within this prison.

No matter what might happen, I'm still on a mission.

All I need is the support of a friend, the devotion of a friend, and the understanding of a friend, even though I'm faced with death. I still need a friend that I can truly and completely trust.

Because I would love to put a smile upon your face; 'Cause friendship is deeper than the word.

And friendship is a word of encouragement when you're feeling down, so all I need is a friend to believe in me because there's still a lot of good left in me.

I would love to touch your soul, even though I might never get a chance to even hold. I still want to treasure it as gold.

I need a friend who's not afraid to be my friend, even though someone might see the flaws that I have.

I just hope that I live to see the stars with you someday because I have nothing but "Kind words For A Friend"!!!!!

LAST RESORT

Suicidal thoughts constantly rack my brain.
Is this the only solution
To relieve myself of this pain?
Is this my last resort?
I don't want to die at my own hand,
But I'm sick of this suffering.
I've no longer got the will to fight.
Can somebody help me, please?
I need some relief.
I'm begging on bended knees.
All I want is a little peace.
I can't take it no more.
I've lost my will to live.
All my strength has been drained.
I have nothing more to give.
I have a razor in my hand.
I'm about to cut my vein.
Can't you people understand
That all I want is to stop the pain?
I'm feeling light-headed;
The blood is flowing fast.
In a minute I will exist no more,
Finally peace at last.

Written in late 2004/2005

THE LETHAL TRUTH

For years, Texas has been executing people, not even knowing if the person they are executing was really guilty or not. And if you look closely at this state, you'll really see that in many ways this is a hate crime state against all minorities and lower classes.

What is wrong with being a different race or class? Nothing, because we're all the same; just a different race and class. Some will say that racism and social injustice played out a long time ago. That isn't true.

Why are so many minorities being convicted for crimes that the state can't find any evidence on, a witness and/or anything tying the minority to the crime? But, will be quick to erase the jury's mind of the innocence that the minority might have.

When they examine a juror in jury selection, why do they tell the juror that the defendant is from a seedy neighborhood? Meaning, the neighborhood is a threat to anyone who visits, and if the defendant lives there, you know that they are going to do the same. Not true at all. Because there have been people who have been raised in Los Angeles, New York, et cetera, and are successful and have never been in trouble with the law.

One thing that's a fact is, you cannot tell a non-minority or someone of a higher class that, because they have already been filled with fear and hate, if the defendant was to be set free, they could be next. The state of Texas always claims that they are fair and give a defendant the benefit of the doubt. If that's so, then why won't defendants make it out after being found to be not guilty and serving half of their useful life in a place like death row?

There are many cases like this, but Texas will execute us before they will let us go. For the fact that they don't like to be wrong, they will hide, misplace, and et cetera anything that proves they are wrong. Then, they go ahead and execute us.

Having the best record of executing someone isn't something to be proud of. These are human beings we are talking about.

Why do they give a drug dealer and/or someone who didn't even have anything to do with a crime the death penalty? Now, I don't approve of drug dealin' or someone's life being taken, but where does murder come in?

Is it because the state has been trying to get the defendant and they couldn't get them?

Why, when they can't get the defendant that they find a person that has something against the defendant, and use them to build a case that they don't have, but the jury will believe them if they can tell them what to say?

Find an ex-spouse or old texts that shows the defendant cheated on them, and use them 'cause they have been waiting for a chance to hurt them, and will say anything the state tells them to.

A scorned spouse in the jury's eyes is the most trusted witness 'cause they feel sympathy for them thinking that they are telling the truth. When, in reality, they are there to make the defendant look bad. They will find people who the defendant doesn't even know, yet they will swear that they do. Then, it comes to light that they don't even know the defendant at all, and when caught up in a lie, the prosecution will ask for a recess; so that they can go refresh their witness's mind.

Then, the judges, attorneys and prosecution work together.

Yes, it might seem as if the attorney is doing all that they can, yet when the defendant asks them to ask questions that will help the defendant, they answer they aren't good enough.

People are convicted of the most gruesome murders, but they aren't on death row, and this is where both race and class plays a part again.

The Texas Chainsaw Massacre (White/Life Sentence). Known for numerous killings.

Charles Manson (White/Life Sentence). He brainwashed a lot of people, and used them to kill others.

Jeffrey Dahmer (White/Life Sentence). Killed many, and then ate them.

I could keep going down the line 'cause there's a lot of them serving sentences for more than just one murder. But, all it takes is a minority or someone of a different class to do the same thing, and without a doubt, they get the death penalty. And, some are first time offenders who were just trying to protect themselves from harm's way and/or were trying to impress someone, but everything went wrong.

They get the death penalty just for being at the wrong place at the wrong time. A person is free to go wherever they please and no one owns anything in many neighborhoods, except in the city. Yet, to some people they think they do, and anyone that comes that way is in danger.

The question is, what would you do if you're out enjoying yourself by taking a walk and/or just trying to relax and get a peaceful mind when someone walks up to you with a gun drawn? You know what they have in mind, but they get too close, and you grab for the gun. Y'all struggle for a while and then the gun goes off. That someone falls to the ground, and now everyone comes out to see what's going on. It doesn't look right, a body on the ground, and you standing over it with a gun. Yet, all those that came out didn't see what really happened, but will tell the police that you just walked up to that someone and killed them.

This is how so many of us end up here. When the prosecution gets finished making you look like a monster, it's easy for them to throw your life away.

Yet, you have people like Oprah, Ellen, and many more who are scared to try and help because if they do interfere, they will be destroyed. Nobody wants to fall from their high horse, but somebody needs to help because people are dying. They just need someone to stand up; to help them fight for what's right. They said at trial that we couldn't be rehabilitated, but there's James V. Allridge III, Joseph Nick-Bey, Anthony Fuentes, Gerald Mitchell and Derrick O'Brien.

Also, there's Derrick Frazier, Dominique Jerome Green, Edward Green, George Andy Hopper, James Jackson, Newton Anderson, Gregory Summers, Tai Chin Pryor and Christopher Young. All these men tried to make a change for the best in their and other's lives because it's never too late to change. People change their ways and lives all the time.

People of America, who cares, please get your hands in the progress of the program and help stop the crazy killing Texas is doing just because of a person's color or class.

Please don't let the next person's blood be on your hands when you know that you can fight to help someone. At least if it still happens, you can say that we tried and kept fighting to help save someone until we win.

Because, believe me, if we stick together we can win this battle, which is almost over in most states, but we need to focus on Texas.

Please. Let's do this, so that we won't have blood on our hands for the rest of our lives.

Stop The Executions!

LIFE

One thing,
We as people,
Have to realize
About life
Is:

Things are going to happen
All the time...

It's not about
What happens in life --
It's
What we do
With
What happens in life...

And
How we allow things
To affect us
Is
Entirely up to us,
And
Will determine
Our outcome
As people
And
Individually...

LOOKING INTO THE EYES
OF AN UNJUST SYSTEM

I remember it as if it was just yesterday: when I agreed to sign a plea agreement. When Chuck Rosenthal (the District Attorney) came and tore it up, yet it wasn't so much of him tearing it up. It was the look in his eyes that said "I got you". Once he tore it up and threw it back at me, the look in his eyes said "Take that". Now, after eighteen years of being on death row, I sit in my cell and replay it over and over just as if it happened yesterday.

This was not the only time that he or the system showed injustice against me. Upon my being arrested, I was taken before a lineup, and I wasn't identified. However, some twenty months later the victim sat upon the witness stand and positively identified me. Now, if that doesn't show prosecutorial misconduct, then I can't explain it.

Now, upon it being time for me to pick a jury for my trial against this injustice, a couple qualified African American jurors were inappropriately struck by a preliminary challenge by the prosecution. So, by the result of that, the cards were stacked against me to the point that there were no African Americans on my jury. And if that wasn't the act of an unjust system on a mission, then I don't know what else to say.

But, I can go even further. When it was around the time I was about to go to trial, a Caucasian male was going to trial for the brutal beating murder of a man that had his head bashed in by this

Caucasian male. Yet, he was given some prison time instead of finishing his trial. But, when I had signed a plea agreement for either sixty years or life, I was denied that chance by an unjust system on a mission. In my opinion, their goal was to get, not only me, but to get all minorities arrested and charged with a crime.

Upon growing up, I never looked at things with an unjust outlook. But now, looking into the eyes of an unjust man and system, I now see things in an unjust light; ever since I was faced with having to fight for my life. As I was on trial for murdering a Caucasian med student, in the eyes of an unjust system, I was just "another law breaker".

MY LOVELY MOTHER

I love you,
And I know that anything
That I say doesn't
come as that big of a surprise.
And I've told you numerous
Times before.

Yet, today seems
As good as
A time as ever
To tell you, Mother,
How much you mean to me.

I love you most of all
Because you are the only
One that's been there through
The good and bad times.

And when it's easy,
And when it takes
You all the patience
In the world to do so.

And know that
Out of all the people
In the world,
You're the only one
I'm glad to have as my mother.

So, "Happy Mother's Day"

MY THOUGHTS ON:
SELF-DETERMINATION

Self-Determination is not something you gain. It's something you use and have to maintain. Throughout these past eighteen years I've been incarcerated, I've learned that a man can have knowledge and the world at his fingertips, but if he has no morals or self-determination he will only self-destruct.

To me, this all starts with trusting in self. To be able to master this, one must have control over their thoughts. And that starts by taking yourself in hand and asseverating over all the details of your everyday life.

Don't allow mind, body and soul to do exactly what it wants to do. Administer your command over those, which allows you to start mastering your own self-control and self-determination.

Because by mastering the proclaimed title, you can always choose your own path without awaiting orders from someone else, and you must demand and expect instant action, instead of trusting in someone else.

So, mastering your own self-determination and trusting in self to guide you will protect you in all your ways of life.

The way to obtain this is to acquire what I call the "Trinity Of Self", which comes through "Productive Progress". The outer rim of this trinity is negativity, turmoil and chaos, and it isn't smart to think outside of this trinity 'cause this trinity is self, and should always approach problems (good or bad; through this trinity of self). This trinity is a training that goes on physically, mentally and spiritually inside of self instead of looking elsewhere for help. Look inside of self for help because all you have to do is believe in this trinity of self, which lies within.

Now, with all that being said, I might be only thirty-eight years old, but I've seen a lot about life. I can speak from personal experience that believing in this trinity isn't soft, friendly, nor weak, but smart. To me, if we showed and acted on this trait the world would be a better place to live. And these are My Thoughts On: Self-Determination!!!

NEVER

Never in my wildest dreams would I have thought that I would ever meet a soul as beautiful as yours.

If someone would've told me that in my future an angel would drop from the sky into my world to try to save it, I wouldn't have believed them, even if they were psychic.

The things you speak of, your thoughts, your beliefs and the hope you give for tomorrow is something that's needed for me to see through the darkness.

If there is indeed "an angelic being" here on earth, then that "angelic being" is you.

And I would have never thought that "angelic being" would come in the form of you, Naomi, a cherished one!!!

Dedicated to my attorney, Naomi Fenwick

ONE DAY TO THE NEXT

I am disappointed
Because today has returned
To look more like yesterday.
But then I realize
That it's more beautiful
Than them all.

When today disappears
Into tomorrow's silvery haze,
I missed the work of the Creator's hands
That has made
These beautiful days.

Then suddenly, it's a new day
All over again,
But with a different hue.
For colors to come
From the ground
With a different mood
Of joy and blue.

And when today once again appears,
I am so thankful and glad
That the Creator has shared
All this beauty with me
Because this beauty is different
From one day to the next.

These days,
Oh, how beautiful they are

Because they give my soul a lift.
They show me how much the Creator loves me,
To give me such a beautiful gift.

OPENED EYES

When I was growing up, I guess you could say that I was one of those kids who was always getting into something. I was hardheaded, but honestly, I wasn't a bad kid. What I was was basic. I was one of those people who had to go through things myself. It seemed that I refused to learn from the mistakes of others. Instead. I went ahead and made my own mistakes. Crazy? Maybe in one sense, but I know without a doubt that learning lessons of life by going through trials and tribulations teaches you the first time. Rarely did I make the same mistakes twice.

It took me a while to realize that it's both unwise and unhealthy to always go through trials and tribulations on my own. Yet, once I figured out what life was, it has been a lot easier. But, it took me being placed within my current circumstances to open my eyes. And with the realization that it's not wise to make your own mistakes. I also learned that at times the lesson puts you into a situation that you cannot get out of.

I am in such a predicament. Because at the age of 19, I made the biggest error of my life by being involved with a robbery that cost a man his life. Now, eighteen years later, I find myself sitting on death row fighting to persevere in my own life.

All of this is because I refused to observe the paths of others. I insisted on paving my own path. I've learned my lesson, and today I observe the paths of others, but this has been a very hard lesson to learn. 'Cause growing up, I was the baby of my family. I didn't have any family who lived by and/or who I was close to. So, I found myself relating more to adults than I did with kids my age. One would expect that because I related to adults more that I would have gained some of their knowledge and wisdom.

I cannot say that I gained nothing. Yet, I can say that I missed out on gaining the much needed knowledge and wisdom that would have made my life less drama filled.

Once I perceived that I should do my best to observe the path of others, I was already incarcerated. From the beginning I was drawn to the older convicts. Of course I spent time with those of my own age, but I noticed that I related to and tried to learn all that those older convicts had to teach me. 'Cause I was facing a new trial and I didn't want to experience the tribulations of incarceration from continuing to pave my own path (But of course in the end I did).

The first convict that I ran into was a man who had been incarcerated for twelve years, and although he was only thirteen years older than I was, he had prison experience, so I tried to gain as much knowledge as I could.

At the age of twenty-one, I was sent to death row and the first friend I had was a 30-year-old man. At the time I ran into him, he had been incarcerated for more years than he had been free.
I guess you could say that I sat at his feet (in a sense) and tried to gain all that I could.

He was executed. But the knowledge and wisdom he gave me remains with me to this day.

Within my years of incarceration, I've been close to numerous "older convicts". I've seen in them what I refused to see before getting incarcerated, and that is that no one goes through life and gains nothing.

Growing up, I thought that my parents, older people, and teachers were out of tune with the time; stuck in the past and/or crazy or senile.

I had the mentality that I knew it all. Boy, was I totally wrong.

I see today that I missed out on gaining so much because I refused to take heed of the path that my elders did.

Maybe if I had someone that I could relate to that was old enough to have experienced the trials and tribulations of life, yet young enough to understand me, maybe I wouldn't be here today.

I can go 'round and 'round about the "If's". Yet that doesn't change the present. I cannot change the past, but maybe it is possible to reach someone and help them realize what I didn't.

It is possible to try and use my trials and tribulations to help someone avoid going down the same path that I did.

I am thirty-eight years old and in such a short time I have seen a lot. I used to think like many youth and adolescents of today think. I thought it was cool to do all the things that my parents, older people and teachers told me not to do. Instead of just enjoying each and every moment of life as it comes. Yet maybe there's someone out there who will read this and reevaluate their life; make a change for the better before it's too late.

It's also possible that I'm coming off like an old man who's out of tune with the time, stuck in the past and/or iust crazy or senile.

And for those few, if I'm still in existence, I'll be there to help you break being unable to see and hear the wisdom.

Either way, it's your life. Live it to your own accord. Yet, I hope that at least someone takes heed of this knowledge and wisdom and changes the path of their life. Prevent yourself from continuing the cycle that myself and many of those incarcerated today were on.

OUR PONDERINGS

Have you ever noticed that the worst way to miss someone is when they are right beside you, and yet you can never have them? The moment you can't feel them under your fingertips, you miss them?

Have you ever wondered which hurts the most: saying something and wishing you had not, or saying nothing and wishing you had?

I guess the most important things are the hardest to say. These are the things you get ashamed of because words diminish them. Words shrink things that seemed timeless when they were in your head...to more than living size when they are brought out...

Don't be afraid to tell someone that you love them. 'Cause if you do they might break your heart...but if you don't you might break theirs...

Have you ever decided not to become a couple because you were so afraid of losing what you already had with that person? Your heart decides who it loves and who it doesn't. You can't tell your heart what to do. It does what it wants on its own when you least expect it or when you don't want it to. Have you ever wanted to love someone with everything you had, but that person was too afraid to let you? Too many of us stay with our walls up because we are too afraid to care too much for fear that the other person doesn't care as much as you do or not at all...

Have you ever loved someone and they had absolutely no idea? Or fell for your best friend and

then stood back and watched as they fell for someone else?

Have you ever denied your feelings for someone because of your fear of losing that person or was rejection too hard to handle?

We tell lies or half truths when we are afraid...afraid of what we do not know...afraid of what others will think...afraid of what will be found out about us, but every time we tell a lie or half truth, the thing we fear grows stronger...

Life and love is all about risks and they require you to jump... Don't be the person who has to look back and wonder what they would have or could have had...

Because Life nor Love waits on no one!!!

OUTCAST

From the dim regions
Whence my fathers came,
My spirit.
Bondage by the body.
Longs.

Words felt,
Never-I-heard,
My lips would frame.

My soul would sing
Forgotten jungle songs.

I would go back
To darkness and to peace.

But the great western world
Holds me in my fee.

And I may never hope
For full release.

While, to its alien Gods,
I've bent my knee.

Something in me is lost,
Forever lost.

Some vital thing
Has gone out of my heart.

And I must walk the way
Of a life,
A ghost.

Among the sons of earth,
A thing apart.

For I was born,
Far from my native kin
Under the white man's menace,
Out of time.

Written on Deathwatch 2015/2016

THE PATH OF AWARENESS

One must understand that in life: whatever decision or choice you make is going to have an action and a reaction. Whatever decision or choice you make (good or bad), you have to stand firm and true, and deal with whatever is dealt your way.

One must understand that in life: to never try to do things by force, and just wait. Whatever you have or had in mind to do will manifest itself.

One must understand that in life: to work in truth always; knowing that when you work in truth, you are helping lead all forms of life into the path of awareness.

One must understand that in life: to never look down or back, nor be worried about the little things that could cause you trouble and disturb your path.

Because one must understand that in life: to always look forward into truth, knowing that truth is working its purpose, which is to lead all forms of life into the path of awareness!!!

PHOENIX RISING

What's good, World, peep the science! I have been throughout these years struggling with the aspects of growth and being willing to destroy what's been built on a rocky foundation.

Why? Some will ask. Because I've thought that I have needed others to be able to maintain. Yet, by having this need, I've brought upon myself a lot of trouble, heartache and pain. To the point where my livelihood was brought into question, and I've been having to choose between what is true and false.

It took my life being actually threatened to be taken before the years of struggling would stop. And once the veil of falsehood was lifted from my third eye, I started to fully understand the message that my real brothers have been trying to instill in me over the years.

Now don't get me wrong, growing and at the sametime, destroying something isn't easy. For me, as a man, it was very prideful; it was extra hard. Yet, this same pride has been the leading force behind my continuing to build onto a rocky foundation and hang on to gangrenous relationships.

So, after me seeing how gangrenous things can be has been the integral pathway to me changing into the man I know I am supposed to be. So, I have to stop living a negative life and do as Corinthians 13:11 says.

Once I got it into my head to stop being afraid to change, things became that much easier for me. Yet, I thought to myself, how can I really want to change and grow when I continue to respond to a name that was the compounding factor to my present demise and restraining me from rising into a Phoenix? So, I've destroyed my present self, and have been born into who I am supposed to be.

From this moment until my descent, I am only going to answer to the name my Old Earth (My Mother) gave me, which is Perry, or my Supreme Being name of Sharif.

Now, I know that I will be ridiculed for being and becoming a true man. But it doesn't matter to me because as with everything that's true, pure and different, we as human beings will shun anything that we don't understand. Just look at what happened to Jesus, Martin Luther King Jr., Malcom X, and John F. Kennedy to name a few. So, I know that you have to be willing to take the bad with the good and vice versa. I say, bring it on! I'm up for the challenge because, like a caterpillar, it has to be that before it can transform into a beautiful butterfly.

So, World, join me in this atmosphere of growth because if I can do it in this realm of negativity where it's easier to do the norm and be like everybody else, I know you can do it. Just be willing to stand true upon your square.

P.E.A.C.E.

What's good, World, it's me again. I was asked why am I doing y'all a disservice by only telling y'all the effect and not the cause.

Well, with that being said, when I first arrived on death row, I was a dreary eyed 21-year-old seeking acceptance in all the wrong places. In doing so, I took on a persona in order to survive. Yet, I didn't know how much indignity that I would face by taking on such a persona. Although, it was from within instead of without.

And when this happened, I remember a brother named Hasan pulling me to the side and asking me, "Why am I allowing another man that bleeds just like you to treat you like an animal?" I was so lost and thought I knew everything, and I didn't see what he was saying. I thought he was trying to run my life, and turn me into who I am supposed to be. He just laughed and said, "Little brother, I am telling you this because I used to be right where you are. I would still have been lost in the wilderness if it wasn't for a brother pulling me to the side. But I see that you are going to have to learn the hard way before you use the knowledge that you have."

That brother actually went to bat for me back here, to try and show me what is true, and I had almost made the conversion into a Supreme Being. But once he was killed, I went back into the wilderness because even though I was strong enough to stand on my own, I didn't think I was. So, like with any set back, a person falls back into what they know best.

Yet, in me falling back on what I have known for so long, I was used as a crash dummy and took on anyone and anything, thinking I had to prove myself. When all I had to do was just tap into my isolated soul.

It wasn't until Egbuno stepped in and diffused a potential life-threatening altercation. He seen something in me that I didn't see in myself, and tried to sit me down and talk to me.

He was, and still is, the only person who calls me Perry, even before I decided to grow up. He looked at me and asked, "Why are you letting that powerful torch of knowledge and wisdom go to waste by being in this wilderness?"

I responded, "What do you mean by wilderness? I am just trying to get it how I live and be the best at what I'm doing?"

He just laughed and said, "By you being an uncharted soul. You have the potential to govern over many. All you have to do is get off the nonsense and be selfish for a change."

"How can I be selfish when I took an oath?"

"I understand that, but how can you be loyal when those that you are being loyal to don't give a damn if you live or die?!"

Even after these talks and wisdom being instilled in me, I still found myself doing like a gerbil, and continued spinning my wheels while going nowhere fast. And as I was going nowhere fast, the hands of justice were moving along just fine with my case going from one stage to the next. I really didn't start paying attention to the crash course my life was on 'til I got inebriated on truth serum for my birthday. Everything that I was feeling came out, and I made a jester out of myself. With that, I knew that I was out of control. But knowing that you are is totally different than seeing that you are.

I was shown that I was by Tai Chin Pryor, a Supreme Being. He took me to the side and asked, "How can you say that you're standing True on your square when your third eye is cloudy?" I couldn't answer because I thought I was standing True…because I had stopped doing a lot of the things that I used to do. Yet, he drove the point home when he said, "By you behaving like a jester, you are making a mockery of the founding fathers of the family that you call yourself representing!"

After that, I sat down and started evaluating my life up until that point. I didn't like what I saw. Because I seen that I have been nothing but someone's puppet, acting without a mind of my own.

Seeing all this caused me to push away, instead of turning to, those that have always had my best interest at heart. I found myself clashing with them to the point where if circumstances were different, I would have had some type of physical altercation with them.

At one point, Ker'Sean, who was more of a brother to me than my own, said, "You trying to get physical with me when I have been the only one who has been there for you as you are going through everything that you've been experiencing.

Why aren't you trying to do the same to those that has been playing you for a fool from day one?!"

That statement stopped me short and started me to really remove the veil of falsehood and see things for what they really are. It was the beginning of the revelation to the path of Supremehood.

His statement hit me harder than anybody else's because he had seen me transform from a caterpillar into a butterfly, and was there through each stage. He didn't have to being that we were the opposite sides of the same coin.

And by being the same coin, we had been able to push each other. By him pushing me, he had helped me build upon a steady foundation; minus the leeches who had been sucking my life force dry.

Even though I saw the truth in everything he had helped reveal, I was still afraid to break free and stand on my own two feet like a man.

It took me receiving an execution date for things to come together and for me to completely spread my wings to take flight. Because of all those that said that they were going to stand with me until the end, only those three and Christopher Young stayed true to their word.

So, once that was shown and proved, I knew that it was time for a change, and to try and help someone else see all that I did not. Yet, instead of talking about it, I have embarked on a Path Of Awareness regardless of what one might think or feel about me. Because "True teaching is not an accumulation of knowledge, it is an awakening of

consciousness that goes through successive stages."
And each stage one embarks on, one must understand that "To know means to record in one's memory; but to understand means to blend with the thing and to assimilate it oneself."

Positive Education Always Corrects Errors

PRODUCTIVE PROGRESS

What's up, World. Just another day in the struggle, but striving and trying to maintain. I need/want you to understand everything I'm about to share with you and take it for what it's worth, because I'm not inferior or superior. Not trying to be anything more or less than what and who I am.

Times and people don't change - some "People" do! But change is detrimental to you because when you change, you drop everything you've ever stood for and believed in. "Maturing" is another thing: 'cause when you mature you tighten up. You take all the positive and negative, and apply it all for progress. So, you can show, prove and tell the blind. My mentality has changed from the ignorant effects of the street lifestyle, and has matured, because I'm about making a difference and making progress; 'cause I am a Poor Righteous Teacher.

One must be willing to go the distance in order to elevate into existence.

I consider myself a Spiritual being, 'cause I have respect for all life. Hate it or love it. I respect it because we all possess a key ~ So, if I knock something that doesn't suit me, instead of reaching on to understanding, I'm no better than my captors. Why scold a blind man if he isn't able to see?

One practical outlook is crucial. Therefore, we must see things for what it is and not for what we want to see. What is normal? Normal is different. That's why we were all created different....Difference is normal. No two minds are alike.

In our culture, yes, we were forced to adapt, but mankind is unique in such a fashion in order to survive. A lion is a lion. A caterpillar matures into a butterfly, but mankind can be anything we put our minds to. We all weren't taken from our land. We were sold by our culture — Why? It goes deeper than the color of one's skin. It is about the color of money "Green" and the destruction of one's land.

Blacks were considered slaves and whites were servants. I am about change and progress. But, I'm a man first, then a Black man. This isn't written to argue or to be disagreed, and I'm just collaborating for understanding in a physical, mental and spiritual way. This is a good exercise for all, because if we allow ourselves to open up and learn, then we manifest into "Productive Progress…"

P.E.A.C.E.

A PROMISE

A force draws near
To a frazzled,
Intergalactic being.

A haven for
A metamorphosis
Messiah.

A consoler
Of metabolism
Views.

Gunforting
Metaplestic
Bonds.

As a true
Meteoric
Reboot
Is born.

Written on Deathwatch 2015/2016

A REFLECTION

I was born to proud and wonderful parents. I have been forever loved and cared for. I wouldn't take anything away from the way I was raised. Yet, I wish I only would have listened to them when they told me that you have no friends and that family comes first; that no one comes before Self and them…because if I would have done so, I feel that I would have saved myself a lot of heartache and pain.

As with any family man, my father spent time with us when he could and taking care of us came first. But, as with most Black people throughout American history, we were financially behind, so he found himself working constantly to try to come out ahead. He tried to make sure we had everything or all the things he didn't have growing up. Most of the time, as I recall, he and my mother went without in order to do so. They didn't want us to dwell on how poor we really were. Yet, in doing so, a few times utilities were cut off. This was not only us, but many families in my neighborhood went through the same troubles.

I know that it might be shallow of me, but even though I had the love of my father and knew that he had to work, I wanted him to constantly be around me and at my school activities the way I saw many other fathers. So, instead of just feeling blessed for even having a father there, unlike a lot of the other boys in my neighborhood, I would go looking elsewhere for this type of love. I had my mother there always, but she couldn't give me the love and attention my father, or any male in particular could, and that I craved.

My craving for a male role model was what led to it being shown that I was gifted at sports. I only played street ball since I went to a form of homeschool due to my mother trying to shelter me from the harsh realities of the street lifestyle that my brother had already fallen victim to. She saved me in many ways, but she also caused me to miss out on learning the many normal lessons of life that I feel I would have needed to succeed in life. Yes, I didn't go through harsh realities of gang and prison life that my brother experienced early on in his life, but it made me develop the mindset that I was untouchable and the same rules in life didn't pertain to me as it did to others. So, I found myself unconsciously living recklessly. Even still, my brother's fate and experience made me not want to go down the same road he did (yet, unfortunately, I did).

Me being sheltered, I couldn't fully tap into my gift being that my school didn't have any type of sports program. So, I talked my parents into (more like had my father convince my mother) allowing me to go to public school (which was a culture shock to my system because it was like I was an alien amongst humans when I seen all the things that I was behind on when it came to life as a kid growing up). And once I hit an organized sports program, my gift flourished, and as it flourished, so did my popularity. Me being a sports star and so popular was both good and bad for me. It brought me the love and attention I craved and females that I wouldn't have ever thought I had a chance with (which was good). Yet, being that I'm such a loner in many ways, I didn't know how to compartmentalize each situation and see the truth of them (which was bad). So, by me not being able to do so, led me to being caught up in drug and gang involvement, and started me down the same road my brother traveled.

A veil was pulled over my eyes by both a friend and a supposed girlfriend to think that being involved with each of those things, 1 would get an unlimited supply of love and attention that I craved. So, I found myself doing whatever I had to do at sports to keep this love and attention. It wasn't until I found myself within my present situation and had time to reflect, that I seen that I was loved and wanted unconditionally no matter what I did.

Yet, coming here where life isn't a certainty has caused me to further reflect on not only life, but my beliefs in general. I've been going through life without really experiencing it as I've chased after so many unwanted and unneeded things.

Chasing those unwanted and unneeded things has caused me to enter into so many unhealthy friendships and relationships that had me being something other than myself because I've craved the feeling of being accepted. Yet, when I faced my own death, I was abandoned by, not only those that I've entered into these friendships and relationships with, but also most of my family. It made me think that maybe I needed to start really putting myself first. But, with any cycle, the chain isn't fully broken until you truly want it to be. We don't truly know who we are until we see what we can do because we have to make visible what, without self, might never have been seen.

For anyone out there reading this, reflect on your life so far, and see if it's the life you really want. As a friend who's presently facing death said: "Work on what I can create for tomorrow. And...if it don't come, it don't come, but that's what I'm going to keep working on." Being that how far you go in life depends on doing what your intended purpose calls for you to do, and not diverting from it, we must use time creatively.

THE ROYAL LAW

Throughout these past 18 years, I have learned that a man can have knowledge and the world at his fingertips, but if he has no morals, he will only self-destruct. If he has no love, he will only wither away. If he has no desire or purpose, he will only make excuses for his failings.

The heart of our problems are the problems of our hearts. Martin Luther King Jr., once proclaimed, "I've seen too much hate to want to hate." Sitting here on Texas death row today, I feel the same way.

There's a higher law-a royal law- on the other side of the law. How others see us is never the true depiction of us, but it is how we see others.

When I think of Tookie Williams, the original founder of the notorious gang, 'The Crips', being nominated for the Nobel Peace Prize for his writing of children's books from a California death row cell...Or Sonny Ray Jefferies, scribing poems, shedding light and creating from a Florida death row cell...I understand the Royal Law of Love is higher than the laws of the state.

I often compare death row to falling deep into the ocean, then rising slowly to the surface, then being asked to tell the story of how you almost drowned. But instead you tell a story of all the hidden treasures you found that no one knew were down there.

Like Dr. King, "I have seen too much hate to want to hate. I have seen too many give up on me to want to give up on others. I have seen and been through too much pain in my life to want to see others in pain".

So, after being labeled a cold blooded killer, being mocked for my beliefs, being defamed by the media, being convicted of Capital Murder, and being sentenced to death, the most beautiful thing happened to me. I had been taken back to a holding tank, and the jailer saw me sitting there as they were coming to take me back to my cell. Breaking the rules, she went and got my family, and allowed my family to hug and spend time with me as they have never done before.

There will always be the Royal Law of Love higher than the laws of the state. I have lived by the Royal Law on the other side of the law where mercy triumphs over judgment.

The state of Texas judges us, believing that judgment is greater than mercy. The death penalty needs to be abolished. No substitutions.

But, if killing me will help prevent someone else from making the same mistakes in life that I have, then I am ready to die. 'Cause if I didn't humble myself, my life has been in vain and over already. There's nothing worse for a man's heart than living in vain or dying in vain. But if we love today, we will never hate tomorrow.

'Cause I have seen too much love to want to hate, and not enough hate to not want to love.

Peace, Love and Respect.

SHOULD'VE BEEN THERE

Ain't no love for the ones
Who didn't stay by my side
When I needed them the most;
that held back from staying down.

And as I roll through this time,
I now know
the feeling of loss.

It's the thought that counts,
But you act like
You've forgotten
that there's 24 hours in a day,
And I ain't even on your clock.

So please stop staring at my picture,
And just let me
Rest with some peace.
Close your eyes and feel the breeze,
And just forget about me.

I'm at peace
At a place
Where there's no such thing as pain,
No more playing games,
And no more crying in chains.

No more stressing,
No more hoping for a visit,
And no more saying "I'm Sorry".

Because when my heart stops
Don't try to act like you care.

And save all of your fake tears
Because
You
Should've
Been
There.

Written on Deathwatch 2015/2016

SOMETHING TO LIVE FOR

At times you may feel that you're damned if you do and damned if you don't, but you are truly mistaken. It's just that our expectations are unrealistic about how life should go for us as individuals. The only thing guaranteed in life for us as human beings is death and struggle while we do live. We will experience both good, bad and/or vice versa. Yes, for some of us, we may experience more bad than good in our lifetime. And most of the time, we do have some type of control over how much of each we go through because some of the negative experience is a result of what we do and how we think. How we think is reflected in what we do, how we live, and how we respond to things.

We were all sentenced to die, but all of us will not end up dying as a result of what we do. Some of us will, yet many many of us won't. So, since we know that death might be our end, this whole experience is more so about how we deal with the possibility; how we choose to live! If we allow death or its possibility to prevent us from extending our hands to others, then we have been defeated by something that is a natural part of our journey. There is nothing unnatural about death.

If we choose to crawl into our shell and turn away from others because they may die, then we are in violation because we have taken away the possibility that they have been put in our path in order to learn some valuable life lessons. A lesson which may be intended for them to pass along to someone else. The chain would be broken and someone will be denied an important lesson because of our selfishness.

Death isn't an enemy. It's an ally who, when the works of life are done for us, just slices the cord that binds us to the earth.

Because of what we have gained from our relationships with others who have transcended, we are hopefully better people, and a truer reflection of what it really means to be a brother and sister! We are their keepers and we should strive to do so to and for those who are still there.

If I was selfish or did not love my people or all forms of life as I say I do, I wouldn't be writing this. If I don't write this, then I would have prevented your growth. And how do I know what it is you may eventually learn from this?! What I'm saying is, it's not just about us as individuals. It's about more than just us. 'Cause just as we had to depend on someone else to assist us in the past when we couldn't provide for ourselves, we have an obligation to do the same for others who truly need and deserve our assistance.

So, we have plenty to live for, obligations to be fulfilled, and lessons yet to be learned. We try, not simply for ourselves, but for others, as well. For those who we care about and vice versa, and for those who still need us.

So, stand true upon your square!!!!!

Peace, Love and Respect.

THE SPIRIT OF LOVE

To love is the spirit
The creator has given
Us within
Without the thought of taking it back.

We're all so struck
On the need to have love returned,
But to truly love
We must learn to love.

Love is a beautiful gift,
Which comes from
The heart
And flows into life.

STANDING TRUE

One thing in life
That you should keep in mind is
That everything has a cost.
Even change-
When we are trying
To change how we live.

When you seek to change,
You will be tested
In all kinds of ways,
Talked about,
Maybe even talked crazy to.

But we have to
Pass the test
In order to
Achieve the change
We seek.

As long as you aren't
Physically attacked,
You got to hold
Your position.

Talk is something
That even the lowest of the low,
The weakest of the weak-
Can do.

Talk don't
Make us
Who we are.

How we live
Reflects who we are.

It takes more strength
To do what's right,
Than it does
To go
with the flow.

In the end,
It's our choice
As individuals
As to
Who we eventually become

STRUGGLE

Struggle
Is the ability
To handle
And
Do
All you can
With
What you have.
In
The time you have
And
In
The place you are at.
Because
In life
We don't stay down forever
Or very long -
'Cause eventually
One wins
As long as
They stand strong,
And continue
To have the will
To struggle
With the understanding
That life itself
Is a struggle...
And,
Without struggle
There can be

No progress...
Because
As long as
You struggle
With a purpose
You will always reach
Your intended purpose
So always remember
In life that
"Thought
Prayer
And Action
= Manifestation".….

TANGIBILITY

Tangibility goes unnoticed.
It's a secret kept hidden.
It remains inside
An expression that for so long
Has been forbidden.

I've stored it in my heart,
A place no one can look.
I've replaced it with tangibles
From all the pain I took.

Tangibility is what you see
So you'll never see the fear.
Yet, you'll hear the teardrops
But you'll never see the tears.

You'll see the wounds from the wars,
Scars from the battles,
An outcasted person kept silent
Like a shadow.

But do you know where tangibility is?

Just close your eyes and guess.
Tangibility is
Knowing what's there.

Written on Deathwatch 2015/2016

93

THAT'S LOVE

The Creator takes face
Of every effort that
You take to correct and perfect
The nature of love...

And understands
Your wins and loses,
But continues
To give you everlasting love.

And if he,
Who is so very beautiful,
So very great in spirit,
Can continue
To give you his everlasting love
In light of all that you do,
Is it so hard
To give love to others?

Because to love is
To give the highest and truest
Within yourself,
To your brother,
Sister,
Mother,
Father,
And friend;
And to love is to give
A part of your soul.

But most of all
The everlasting love of the Creator:

That's Love!!!!!

TOGETHER AS ONE

My life has been rearranged-
Minus not having love,
Equals have changed.
Steadily searching for better things
As I bathe in glorious love.

I cleanse myself daily,
But most importantly,
I love as I'm loved.

I must love by example
To show what it means to be in love,
Which includes humbling myself;
Showing those
Without love
That there is love.

I fight spiritually against
Being afraid of love
Because it's easier to forget and denounce.
So, like a fire drill,
I make sure I run to
Cherish and love you.

Because now that the time has come,
I'm not taking any chances.
So I'll always love you
Because not loving you
Is worse than the damage
Done by 39 lashes.

So, our service
We will attend
And love we would never offend.

So, always be sincere from the heart
Because being in love
You can never pretend.

It's not an easy walk
Because, for our love we will
Suffer and fight anything.
We will be ridiculed
Like many before us.

S, whenever someone tries
To speak down about our love,
Just cut them off
And tell them to shhhhh.

Because a new beginning
And a new life
we share
"Together as one".

TRINITY OF SELF

The way to truth is by obtaining the Trinity Of Self through Productive Progress. The outer rim of this trinity is negativity, turmoil and chaos. It isn't smart to think outside of this trinity 'cause this trinity is self and you should approach problems of life (good or bad) through the Trinity Of Self.

This Trinity of Self is a training that goes on physically, mentally and spiritually. Instead of always looking elsewhere for help, look inside of self for help because all you have to do is believe in this Trinity of Self, which lies within.

TRUTH BE KNOWN

Truth Be Known...
When we first met, I knew that we'd be together and our love's fire would forever remain lit. The truth was made when our souls stole their kiss.

Truth Be Known...
I knew I loved you before I even uttered those words, but I tried to run from the feeling. Our love's magnetic energy was stronger than my resistance, though — I found myself embracing our love readily and willingly.

Truth Be Known...
When we feel in love, it was a reunion for lovers from a previous life who expressed their love and longing for each other.

Truth Be Known...
I'm attracted to your whole being (mind, body and spirit) and I love the beauty of what you represent. True love, loyalty, respect, growth and strength.

Truth Be Known...
Our brief history, time and distance has shown and proved that U.N.I. have an UNION that can't be broken. It has been said that everything began with a word. Well, I believe U.N.I. was created by the Most High when the word "Love" was first spoken.

Let This Truth Be Known...

That it's because I know self that I'm able to see you for who you truly are, a goddess made for my god. The earth rotating around my Sun, the Moon to my Star.

Truth Be Known...
That life transcend through the connection we've made and forever it will complete us.

THE TWO FACES OF JUSTICE

As the Appeals Court of Texas in Austin was affirming Reverend Clarence Lee Brandley's case, another death penalty case also was being affirmed. I wonder how the judges could overlook important issues that could have possibly changed the opinion of the jurors in that death penalty case had they the opportunity without granting a death penalty conviction to a middle aged woman who was on her way to work; a reversal regarding the same jury issue. Example: The judges decided to justify the state's version of the case by citing mediocre factors in this death penalty case while disregarding major factors such as expert testimony that (if allowed) would have probably rendered a different verdict. They reversed the latter citing the jurors' inability to hear testimony regarding the deceased victim's past.

Though these cases differ only on specific points, the basic issue is still the same. The judges in this death penalty case stated that the witnesses were (supposedly) acquainted with the defendant. This was enough to justify affirming the case while ignoring physical evidence, such as ballistics and fingerprints. Both came back negative where the defendant was concerned, and included testimony of several expert witnesses.

One of them was an expert in architectural work who drew a scale of the line up to show how suggestive it was, but because he had no prior knowledge of the defendant's (death penalty) case, his testimony was never heard. The Appeals Court elected to overlook that issue, as well.

The other expert witness was a well-trained psychologist who was willing to testify regarding the identification, but was also conveniently overlooked by the appeals court judges because they knew that such testimony could possibly render a different verdict, especially since the defendant's identification came into question.

Nevertheless, convicted killer and ex-police officer, Alex Gonzeles' case was reversed because the past history of the victim was not allowed for the jurors' consideration.

It seems that whenever a police officer murders a poor member of this society, whether it's in Texas, Detroit, New York or anywhere, the appeal courts always find legal violations that reverses their cases while affirming other cases with similar or the exact same violations. Yet, nobody sees any problem with that as long as it is not some highly profiled individual.

There are other questions regarding the defendant (and a great many others) regarding the grand jury selections where one does not have a right to be present while accusations are being made against you. However, you have a right (under the legislative laws of this state) to challenge the accusations at the grand jury level before an indictment is made, especially where there's controversy regarding the evidence, eye witness statements, etcetera. Nevertheless, these laws are violated on a continuous basis (as it was in the defendant's case), even though the grand jury did not convene to decide on whether to indict or not because nothing was ever presented to a grand jury in the defendant's case (from an evidentiary standpoint or eyewitness testimony).

The district attorney or his assistant simply read off an already prepared indictment and the foreman of the grand jury stamped it (had that dismissed in court). Had the grand jury done as the law states, then the defendant and many others would have never been indicted on either cases because there wasn't probable cause to arrest him. So, what happened to his supposed legislative right under the law of this state?

I'll tell you what happened to them: they were never intended for him (or anyone who has to rely on the state to provide their crisscrossed form of justice).

The judges in the Appeals Court of Austin, Texas have disregarded this entire issue since the beginning of time by making the defendant and many others into scapegoats by the system.

This system takes people from disenfranchised neighborhoods, and with carefully designed tactics and aid of the media, depict us in such a manner that makes the very people that came out or still live in those neighborhoods hate themselves.

This makes it all too easy to rob us of our youth (whether justified or not), then turn around after decades of imprisonment and murder us in the name of this same TWO FACED SYSTEM OF JUSTICE in a Public Relations Ploy to suggest to the mass public that everybody agree with this insane practice by calling it justice.

Now the issue of a woman being put to death comes to light, not simply because she is a woman, but more so that she (like others) has found a purpose in her life which makes her better than she was. That scares the politicians more because it's a direct argument against the future dangerousness that has falsely sent a lot of people to death row and/or to an early grave…all in the name of justice.

The tenet of that woman's religion was shown to be genuine and should have never been questioned by one who claims to be a good shepherd. He's really a wolf in sheep's clothing (speaking in regards to the state hired employee that chants scriptures from the Bible to people before they are injected with suffocating poisons).

The myth of this procedure being painless is absurd. To think that the chemical fed through an intravenous tube, a compound form of Pancuronium Bromide, which collapses your lungs, is alright. There's nothing alright with suffocating to death.

At the present, there have been numerous reported "botched" executions and the above has been known to slip out of one's veins, paralyzing the person while at the same time suffocating that person to death (in sophisticated terminology it's called asphyxiation).

Since it is believed to be so painless, then it should be placed on every news station as it is being carried out "LIVE", especially since it is claimed to be (statistically) overwhelmingly supported by the citizens in the state and country (not to mention the extra preparations made to accomodate the victim's family). The voting public should have the opportunity to see their tax dollars at work.

The public sees more violence and death on television everyday (now with the citzen unrest and common murders). This violence is treated as normal by the citizens in this country, so why cop out with petty excuses to not air live executions?

They brag about how proud this state is on being tough on crime and executing people, so surely there should be no argument against airing a live state-sanctioned murder that is so overwhelmingly supported by every citizen in this country.

When our countrymen allow its legal practitioners to practice biased laws against certain citizens, it always hides what it is too shameful to admit to (which this country has a history of doing).

Murdering this woman or anybody for that matter wouldn't change this country's image, nor would it show equality in a system that practices hypocrisy through the aid of most judges along with attorneys, politicians, the media and others.

This only shows that these practitioners will stop at nothing to gain personal fame, which clearly shows: *THE TWO FACES OF JUSTICE* (Revenge American Style).

AN ULTIMATE REALITY

The time has come for me
To end this journey,
And for dusk
To set from dawn.

No tears shed - Why should there be!

When I'm going home
To the universe
Where my soul can
Meditate and be set free.

It's alright to miss me,
But not for long
'Cause I'll be reborn.

So, reflect
On the cipher
We've built

With the knowledge,
Wisdom,
And understanding
Of a Supreme Being.

As my soul is reborn
Into your
Ultimate Reality.

Written on Deathwatch 2015/2016

UNKNOWN TIMES

Creator, please forgive me for all of my faults
'Cause I am not perfect.
No one on this earth is.
I am just trying to love you
How you love me.

Yet, now I see that it was really worth it,
So thank you for being there for me
And bringing me through my dark days
When I faced death within these walls.

For your love I give you all the thanks,
And praises for never turning your back-
For experiencing the possibility of death with me
Then bringing me back.

I thank you for making me the person I am today,
For experiencing the "Unknown Times" with me,
And then showing me how blessed I really am.

You promised to love me
And never allow me to be without.

With you on my team
They can hate it or love it
Because you're going to ride with me
When I'm faced with death or living life
Or even when my back is up against the wall.

With the state of Texas harassing me
And trying to take my life,
It is you who's there with me.

So, through these "Unknown Times“
You've helped me hold my head high
and never stop fighting.

So, until I'm carried out
And they burn my body,
I'll always know that you'll
Stand true with me in these
“Unknown Times“!!!!!

WHY IS EVERYBODY CONDEMNING ME?

Was it I who started the world's deadliest sin? Everybody heard the story told or am I simply a commodity mortified by a twist of fate, yet, a worthless commodity the world should hate?

Why must I be the blame for every ill taken place? Could it be that the clothes I wore and the music I listened to put me in harm's way when the bells of freedom were supposed to have rung…while all my pleas and cries for justice sustain me for only one day.

I sit in a nightmare, hellish is it's bounds-turning towards a light that's not even there. Voices all around me, yelling and banging. And when I try to run away and be by myself, I only turn to the pain that's bare.

Can any of you imagine awakening in an endless hell? No fire, no storms, only suffering and abuse where your nights are illusions of things your heart so longs for…as your thoughts become numb by the eerie drips of lethal injection.

What demons am I really fighting against? The unseen ones that truly lurk in the dark? Omens of wonder, yet time keeps passing by with broken dreams of trust that's so far been manifested.

Sometimes I ponder what the hell I was born for. I had no name, nor a reality I could see. Only unforeseen foolishness that said I didn't belong to a world of neglect and freakish wannabes.

I, too, was once deceived by the display of words like Life, The Pursuit of Happiness and Liberty, Home of the Brave, Land of the Free…So, explain to me, why is everybody condemning me?

I sit waiting for death because society is told that someone has to be blamed. Yet, you who condemn me will accept this as fact with your crosses and hoods reading the bible with no shame.

I ponder at how many of you have ever sinned: one, maybe two. How many of you did wrong? Whether you lied, cheated, stole a few cents, but you now hide behind a title as you cast many stones.

If I was an angel or holier than thou…or maybe even a saint like the one that this world was built on, would you rush to put a needle in my arm? Or perhaps look into the circumstances surrounding me and reverse an unjust decision?

For, I see now that I'm only guilty of being born to who I am in a world where hate is law and murder is wrong for one…Yet, with a license, is sanctioned by another. But, even still, I can't understand "Why Is Everybody Condemning Me"!!!!!

YESTERDAY, TODAY AND TOMORROW

Yesterday, I was with you. Such joy and love we shared because I never knew that my new life would come so quickly. But the bliss I enjoy has surrounded me so sweetly.

Today, I am absent from you, fret not of my end. I was prepared and now I am in the presence of my Creator where my soul awaits judgment, and my heart awaits to Sing.

Tomorrow, we'll be together again, and your hearts will be no more in despair. We will all raise above the darkness and a brighter day will be there to see. We shall all hold hands with Allah and in heaven we'll live eternally.

So, for yesterday, be thankful. For today, be encouraged in faith and remember tomorrow is just a day away. Soon we'll be face to face.

I Love You, Jasir
Always and Forever
Your Brother Perry
7/17/18

Perry wrote this poem the day Chris Young/Jasiri was murdered by the State of Texas; it was Chris who stopped Perry from committing suicide before! Chris also wrote a book called **"My Experience"** which was published posthumously.

UNTITLED 1

Life operates
On the basic principle
Of economics.
"Everything has its cost.
We pay to create our future.
We pay for the mistakes of the past.
We pay for every change we make...
And we pay just as dearly
If we refuse to change."!!!!!

UNTITLED 2

A Supreme Being
Resides in you
Allowing all things
To be renewed.

As you become conscious
Of this congregational
Spirit
That's lying within.

Transcending
Beyond all
Aspects of
A normal being-

When a
Psychodynamic
Change
Is
Born.

Written on Deathwatch 2015/2016

UNTITLED 3

Terrified
Of the unknown-
Terminal tendencies
Of temperamental
Tensions.

Yet,
Terms
Of membranous
Persuasions.

While a permutation
Of perpetual
Piths
Persist.

Written on Deathwatch 2015/2016

UNTITLED 4

Understanding
Has to be worked at
'Cause reactions
To events and conditions
Brings about
Attunements and achievements.

When at times
It's not good
Listening to others
'Cause it could
Hinder you
From
Reaching
Your intended purpose.

As the work
Begins
With self-awareness-

Which is the light
From within
That helps you
Maintain
With all
The conditions
And circumstances
Of understanding.

UNTITLED 5

I recently learned that there is, and if it's true, there will always be a person who will love and care for you. A person who's far away, but always near...

A person that will comfort and console all your sorrow and despair. A person who will give you strength and hope in all the problems that you bear…

A person to turn to for help in distress because when all seems lost or in vain, there's a person you can turn to to bring you confidence and help in reaching your intended purpose...

That person that loves and cares about me without a shadow of a doubt: Is Lotus, my cherished angel from heaven above!!!!!

UNTITLED 6

Becoming aware
Is to live-
Which is:
Free,
Holy,
Happy,
Healthy,
And most of all
Joyous.

Yet firstly,
You have to give
Serenity
To your spire
And let nothing
Impede your way.
Because when you allow
Aspects
To impede your way,

You dispatch
Yourself from
Your transcribed
Manuscript.

So, keep transparent
Of the
Trials and tribulations
That's projected
Your way.

UNTITLED 7

Life is a transition of time
where nothing is for certain
until the end of the spectrum.

Because life is what you
make of it and will reveal
the treasures that the spectrum
has in store for you
or those that matter..

UNTITLED 8

What is pain?
Pain is the feeling that
shows us that we are still
a important line
in the hands of time.

Which the wheel of life,
will provide the answers
needed to deal
with the pain we feel.

So, what is pain?

UNTITLED 9

Words already spoken
And has professed
Your heart's content

Of the sweetest
And best gift
You could ever
Dream of

As your body,
Mind,
And soul
Becomes one

Of the amazing
And wonderful
Attributes
That will never fade.

Written on Deathwatch 2015/2016

UNTITLED 10

Walking through the wilderness of my heart, I'm now seeing a sprout of life that wasn't there a month or even a year ago. It is emanated by your will. I now feel alive in its midst as the aroma of flowers fill my lungs.

The butterflies, larks, honeybees and hummingbirds glide about through the summer breeze.

Leaving behind a sentiment of peace and harmony, which reminds me of the connection we have with our Creator.

This floods my mind with thoughts of you and your words of love. I will try to tap into your energy and mold us together as one being.

With each and every closing of my eye lids, visions begin to flash; the chance to have you as a true friend and beyond brings about a joy in my life, which must be what the Angels in Revelations spoke of, so feel free to emerge oneself with me as one and the same.

UNTITLED 11

A transition
Of time as
Greater unknowns
Are waiting to be found.

Memories of the past
Hold our mind
As we transcend
To the links
Of placid time.

Joyous views
Of empty treasures
As life
Continues to jolt.

Written on Deathwatch 2015/2016

UNTITLED 12

This situation has
My life and heart
Very heavy,
With the
Problems of
These days.

For it has been
A time of
Trials and tribulations.

To a struggle
Of dismay
Because at times
It seems
That all my cries
Go unanswered...

And comforts
My despair
And brings me
The blessings from the
Creator.

Because faith
Comes from
Letting go.

Written on: ll/24/18, I was reflecting, so I guess it opened the floodgates.

UNTITLED 13

Many adventures
Await us upon
The
Road of life.

As to our lives
Isn't but a shadow
Of the one true life.

So, enter
And take
The first step...

Because this is
A journey,
And with every
Step
We reach
A point
Of no return-

Which is
The
Realm
Of
Knowing
Self.

Written on 11/24/18

UNTITLED 14

Pride blinds us
To the need
For change.

Therefore,
For us
to walk the
Path to
True wisdom

We must
Enter
By
The
Gate of humility.

Written on 11/24/18 when I was reflecting on change.